Holiday Joy in the Hudson Valley

Phyllis McCabe

By
Phyllis A. McCabe

ISBN: 0-9716404-2-4

1st Printing 2004

Printed in China.

For additional copies of this book or individual photos,
call Phyllis McCabe at (845) 331-2084 or write to her at
131 West Chester Street, Kingston, NY 12401.

NOTES AND ACKNOWLEDGMENTS

The holiday season in the Hudson Valley is a magical time. Mother Nature clothes the landscape with a quiet and mild light that acts as a backdrop for all the festivities about to come. Store windows in the numerous towns are dressed in their best and boughs of greenery sway from the street lights. The public mansions are decked out in their finery, from the children's Christmas trees to the tinsel on the shimmering chandeliers. Families are sipping hot cider after cutting down their tree at the many tree farms and children are rehearsing their lines for their role in holiday plays.

I have tried to capture some of the essence of Christmas in this book. It was fun traveling around the area and photographing the towns and events. One of my favorites was taking photos of the children's plays and ballet. I loved being in the midst of the excitement and being behind the scenes photographing the rehearsals that took many months to learn. The estates in Dutchess and Putnam counties were a challenge for me to shoot but rewarding. Some of them were only lit by candlelight or window light in keeping with the historic nature of the building.

This book came about when I decided to publish a trilogy after my first book, *To Kingston, With Love*, was completed. Ulster County was my second subject with the resulting *Uniquely Ulster*. Then to broaden my area of perspective, I wanted to do a photographic essay on the Hudson Valley next. Recently there have been numerous books on this subject and I narrowed the theme down to Christmas since it has not been done before.

I would like to thank Pat Murphy for her untiring and invaluable assistance. Without her wonderful insight, this project would not have come to fruition. She is my right hand. Also, I want to thank Jason Zhang for his expertise and attention to detail in the printing process. His artistic eye is evident throughout the book. The curators at the various estates were very helpful and kind in allowing me to roam throughout their charges. Last, but certainly not least, a special thank you goes to Amy Ryan for her intercession in allowing me to fulfill a long-time dream of photographing backstage at the ballet.

Phyllis A. McCabe

Dedication

This book is dedicated to Howard C. St. John, whose vision, commitment and philanthropy defined him as a unique community leader in the Hudson Valley.

Friends of Historic Kingston Museum and the Old Dutch Church, Kingston

Hosanna!

"Chrismas Eve was a night of song that wrapped itself about you like a shawl. But it warmed more than your body. It warmed your heart.. filled it too, with a melody that would last forever."

Bess Streeter Aldrich

Christmas Eve Services at the Old Dutch Church, Kingston

Christmas Eve Services at the Old Dutch Church, Kingston

Trinity Evangelical Lutheran Church, Kingston

Nº 9 Herbei, o ihr Gläubigen
Lebhaft
1. Her - bei, o ihr
CANTIQUE de NOEL
Smoothly

Mount St. Alphonsus, Esopus

Holy Cross Episcopal Church, Kingston

Hurley Reformed Church, Hurley

The French Church, New Paltz

Fair Street Reformed Church, Kingston

St. John the Evangelist Episcopal Church, Rhinebeck

United Methodist Church, Glenford

Vanderbilt Mansion, Hyde Park

Great Estates

"Deck the halls with boughs of holly,
Fa, la, la la la la la la la"

Deck The Halls

Olana, Hudson

Clermont State Historic Site, Clermont

Montgomery Place, Annandale-on-Hudson

Wilderstein, Rhinebeck

Vanderbilt Mansion, Hyde Park

Franklin D. Roosevelt Museum and Library, Hyde Park

Val-Kill, Hyde Park

Staatsburg State Historic Site, Staatsburgh

Locust Grove, Poughkeepsie

Boscobel, Garrison

UPAC, Kingston

Making Spirits Bright

"Christmas is not a time nor a season, but a state of mind. To cherish peace and goodwill, to be plenteous in memory, is to have the real spirit of Christmas"

Calvin Coolidge

Michael's Candy Corner, Kingston

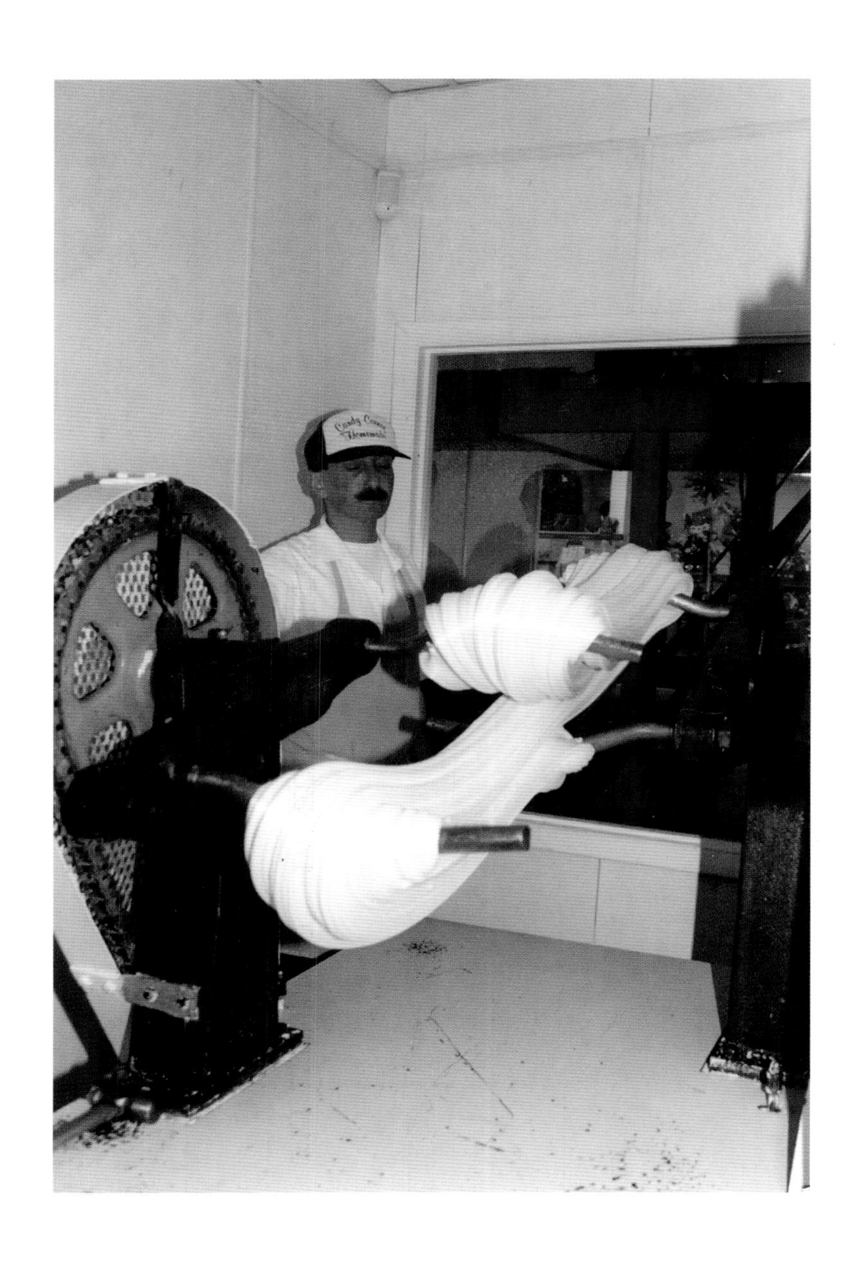

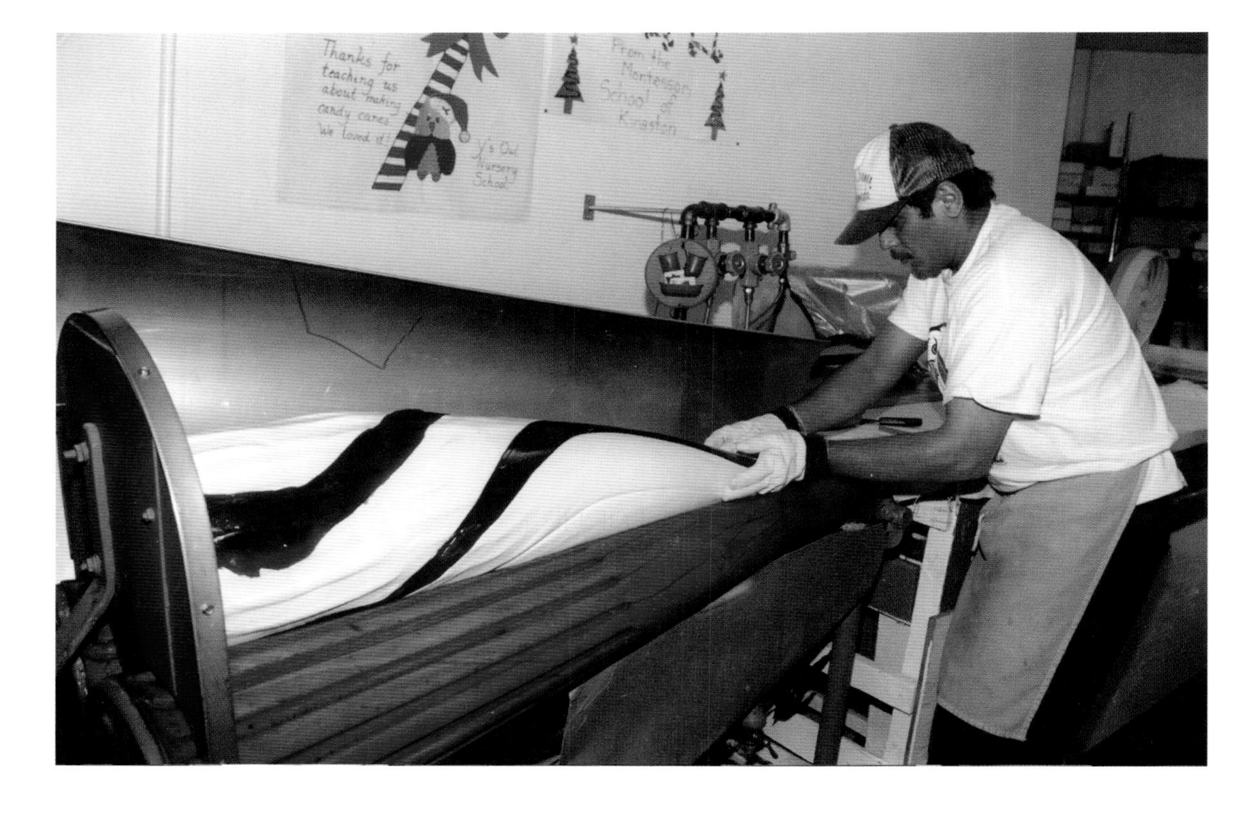

HANDMADE
HANDMADE
Candy Cane
Chocolate Dipped

Battenfeld's Christmas Tree Farm, Rhinebeck

Wallkill View Farm, New Paltz

The Green Cottage, High Falls

Phoenicia

Battenfeld's Christmas Tree Farm, Rhinebeck

Santa Sightings

"No Santa Clause! Thank God he lives, and he lives forever. A thousand years from now, Virginia, nay, ten times ten thousand years from now, he will continue to make glad the heart of childhood."

Francis P. Church

Daisy's Home at 131W. Chester Street, Kingston

Red Hook

The Soyer Residence, Kingston

Ulster County Courthouse, Kingston

Depuy Canal House, High Falls

Kingston Tree Lighting Ceremony

American Legion Post 150, Kingston

St. Mary's School, Kingston

American Legion Post 150, Kingston

St. Mary's School, Kingston

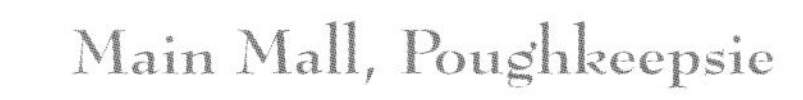

Main Mall, Poughkeepsie

Phoenicia

Dress Rehersal of "The Nutcracker" by the Catskill Ballet Theatre Company at UPAC, Kingston

Great Performances

"I played my drum for Him, par um pum pum, I played my best for Him."

The Little Drummer Boy

Dress Rehersal of "*The Nutcracker*" by the Catskill Ballet Theatre Company at UPAC, Kingston

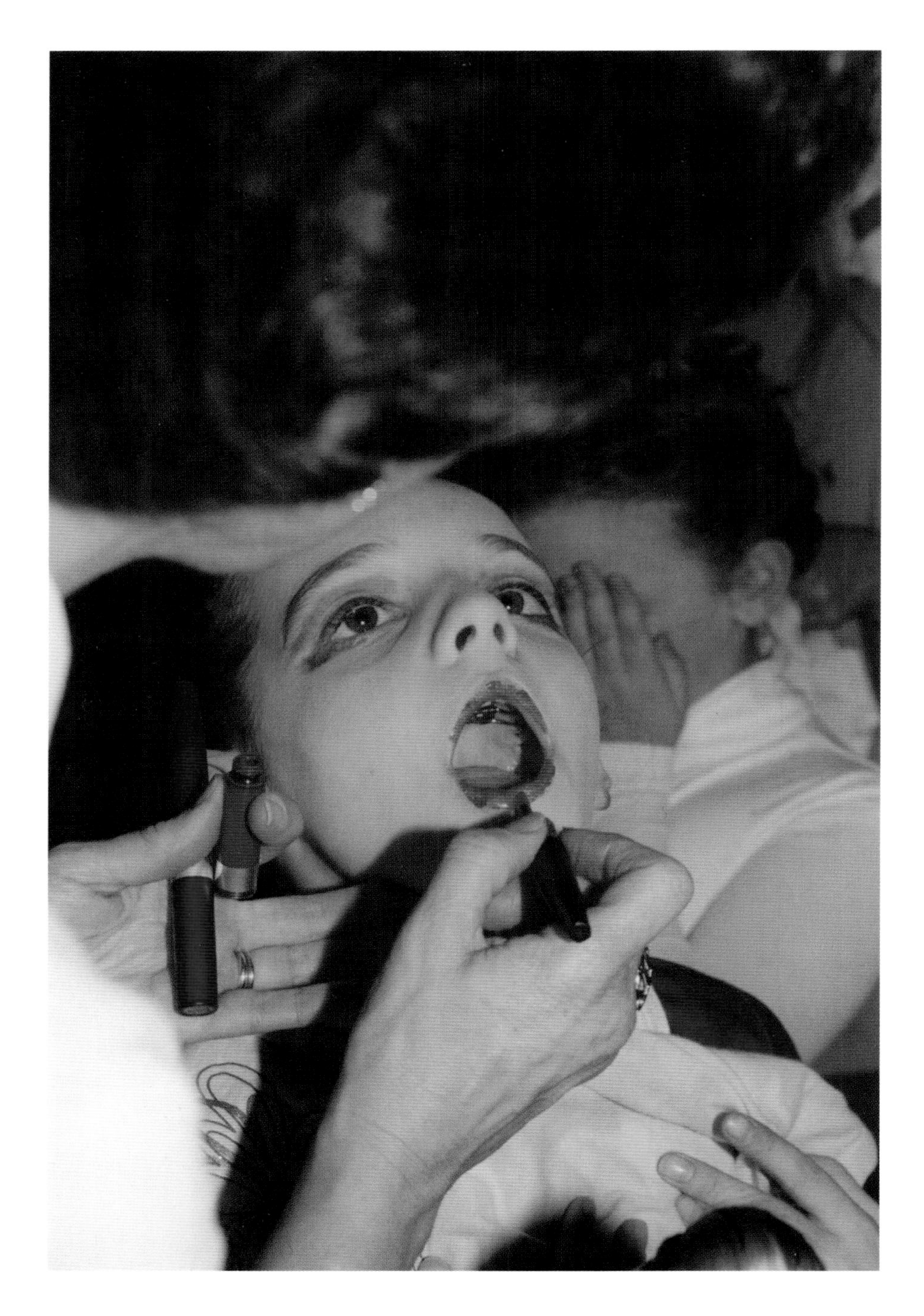

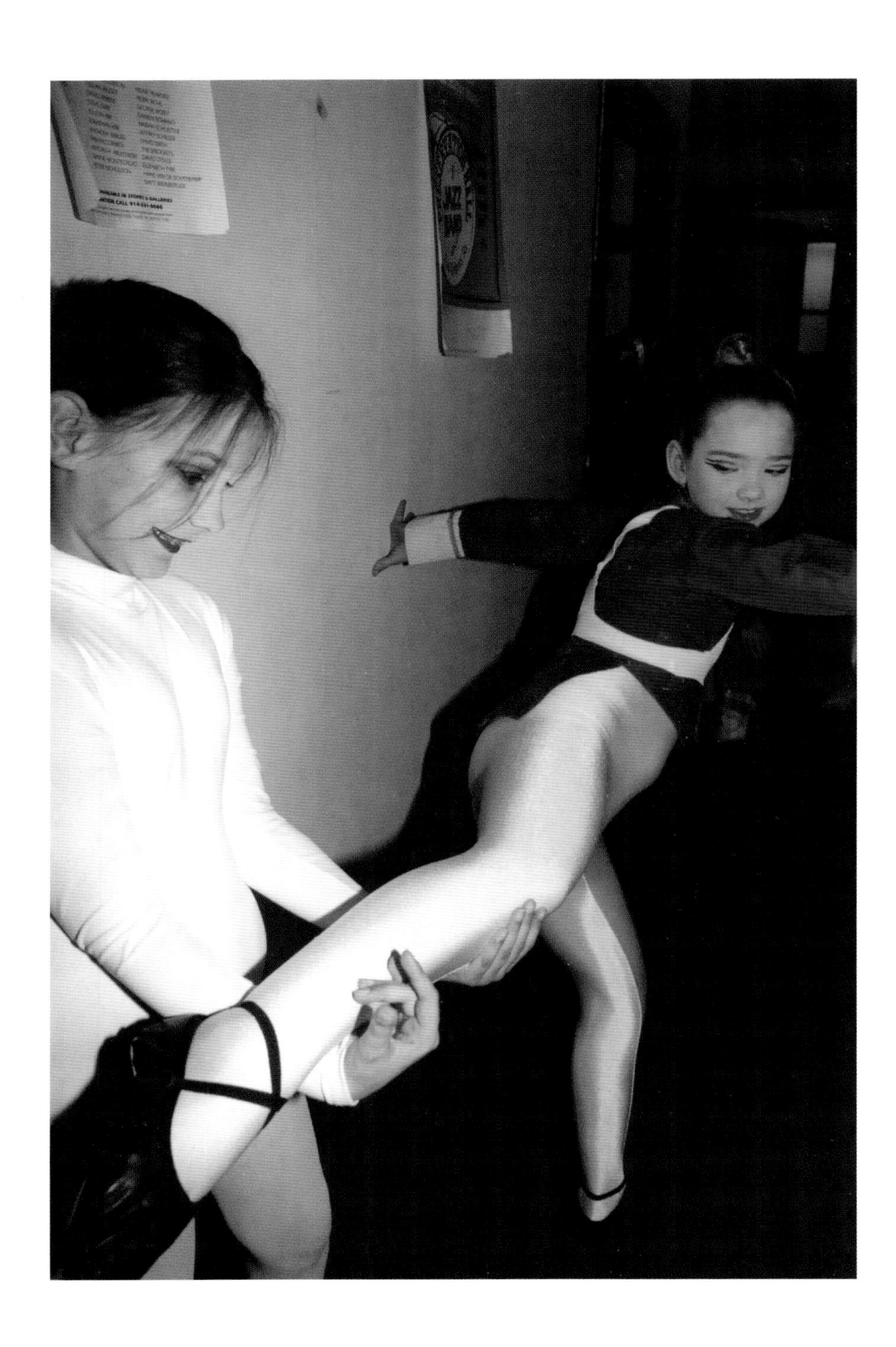

The Bard College Community Orchestra at the Richard B. Fisher Center

Celebration of Lights Parade, Poughkeepsie

"The Littlest Fir Tree" by Director Cara Cruickshank, Phoenicia

"The Littlest Fir Tree" by Director Cara Cruickshank, Phoenicia

"The Littlest Fir Tree" by Director Cara Cruickshank, Phoenicia

"The Living Nativity" at the Old Dutch Church, Kingston

Candlelight Tours at the Senate House, Kingston

Christmas Past

"It comes every year and will go on forever. And along with Christmas belong the keepsakes and the customs."

Marjorie Holmes

Candlelight Tours at the Senate House, Kingston

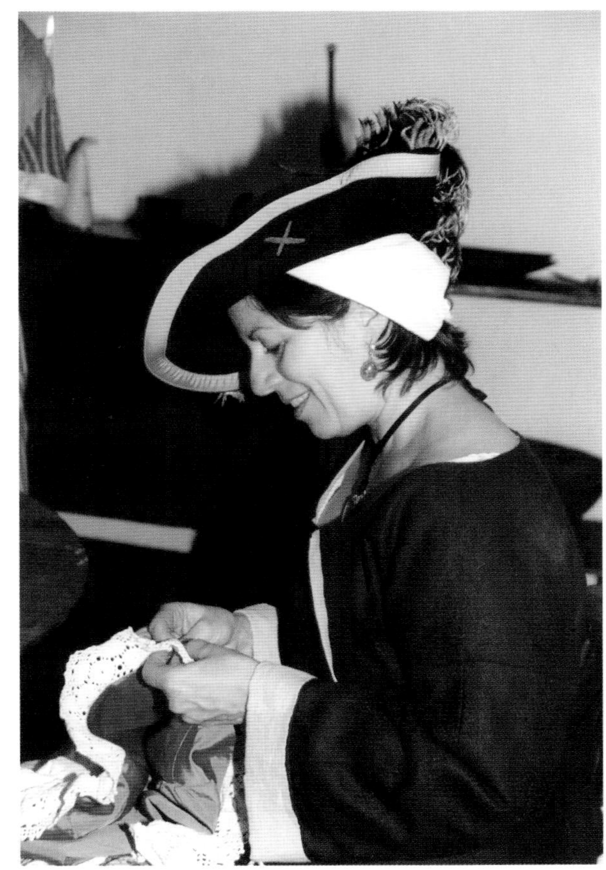

Candlelight Tours at the Senate House, Kingston

Depuy Canal House, High Falls

Roggin House, Kingston

Roggin House, Kingston

The Gilligan Residence, High Falls

The Soyer Residence, Kingston

Houses Great and Small

"Christmas..is not an eternal event at all, but a piece of one's home that one carries in one's heart"

Freya Stark

The Soyer Residence, Kingston

Beekman Arms, Rhinebeck

Mohonk Mountain House, New Paltz

The Delamater Inn, Rhinebeck

Emerson Place, Mt. Pleasant

Woodstock

Ms. Ellen's Annual Tea Party, Hurley

Winterset, Stone Ridge

Staatsburg

The Green Cottage, High Falls

Staatsburgh State Historic Site

Seamon Park, Saugerties

Holiday Lights

"Perhaps the best Yuletide decoration is being wreathed in smiles."

Unknown

Celebration of Lights, Poughkeepsie

Seamon Park, Saugerties

Saugerties Diner

Rhinebeck

ESTAURANT &
CREAM PARLOUR

Winter Sun
Gifts and Clothing
from Around the World

Wall Street, Kingston

The Strand, Kingston

Woodstock

Woodstock

Emerson Place, Mt. Pleasant

Kingston

Window Shopping

"If there is no joyous way to give a festive gift, give love away."

Unknown

Cold Spring

Kingston

Red Hook

High Falls

Mt. Pleasant

Kingston

Red Hook

Hudson

Catskill

Woodstock

Kingston

Rhinebeck

Kingston

Rhinebeck

Kingston

Rhinebeck

Rhinebeck

Kingston

Woodstock

Rhinebeck

Stone Ridge

Peace on Earth

"Christmas waves a single wand over this world, and behold, everything is softer and more beautiful."

Norman Vincent Peale

Hurley Flats

Hurley

Woodstock

Hudson River in Kingston

New Paltz

Kingston

Hudson River from Wilderstein

Wallkill River in New Paltz

Peace on Earth

"I will honor Christmas in my heart, and try to keep it all the year."

Charles Dickens, Ebeneezer Scrooge, A Christmas Carol